A Gift For:

From:

Editorial Director: Carrie Bolin
Editor: Megan Langford
Art Director: Chris Opheim
Designer: Mark Voss
Production Designer: Dan Horton

ISBN: 978-1-59530-664-7
BOK2151

Printed and bound in China
OCT14

Reach
for the
Stars

NOTHING CAN STOP A DREAMER LIKE YOU

now is the time . . .

. . . the time to wonder,
the time to hope,
the time to *dream*.

Now is the time
to look ahead to a future

full of adventure and

opportunity . . .

. . . and all the *best*
that life has to offer.

Whether you realize it
or not, you're a pretty
sensational person.

In a world where
a lot of people
settle for the ordinary . . .

you reach for the
extraordinary.

You've got your own *style,*
your own sense of self.

You know who you are
and where you've come from.

And you can go *anywhere* and be anything you want.

But remember, don't be afraid
to take risks and try new things.

When you go out on a limb
and say, "This is my dream,"
the universe rushes in
to help it happen.

It is as if the perfect coincidences,
the right opportunities,
the absolutely vital information
have all been waiting
for you to make your *move.*

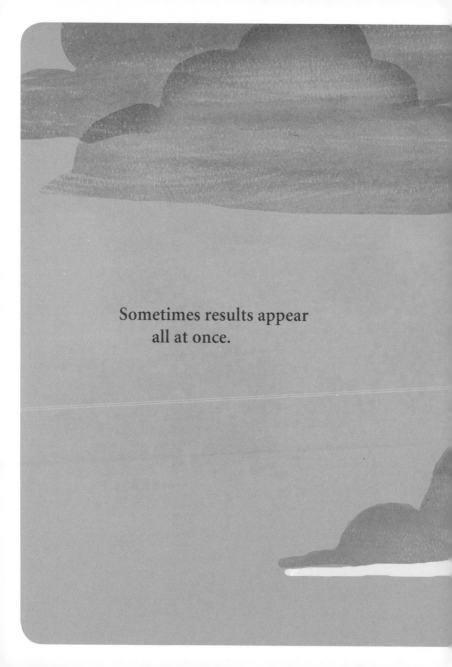

Sometimes results appear
all at once.

At other times, they trickle in
gradually and gently.

It takes *faith* and a genuine desire to step out onto that limb.

But once you're ready
and you make that choice . . .

nothing can stop your *dream*
from coming true.

It is only when you *stretch*
your boundaries that
you can grow and discover
what you'd really like to do
and who you really are.

DREAM

Big.

Be *happy.*

Never compromise on the things
that really *matter* to you.

This is your life.

Make it what *you* want it to be.

Dream your own *dream*
and follow your own star.

There wouldn't be a sky
full of shimmering stars
if we were all meant to wish
on the *same* one.

There will always be *dreams*
grander or humbler than your own . . .

but there will never be a dream
exactly like your own,
for you are *unique*
and more wondrous
than you know!

Do your *best*.

There are *no shortcuts*
on the way to a dream.

Give all that you have
to all that you do.

And above all things,
believe in yourself.

You are as *amazing*
as the stars themselves.

You make a place for yourself in the world,
growing more confident each day.

You work hard.

You face difficulties
with determination and *confidence.*

You're a *winner* . . .

not because you never lose,
but because you are always
willing to give it a try.

No matter what happens
today or tomorrow . . .

you'll come out on *top*.

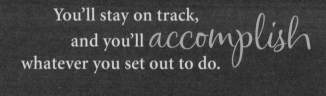

You'll stay on track,
and you'll *accomplish*
whatever you set out to do.

Imagine all your *tomorrows*
as empty pages for you to fill any way you desire.

What dreams will become real?
What surprises will find you?
What stories will you live?

Imagine the future you want . . .

Just be *yourself*, and reach for the stars.

Nothing can stop a *dreamer* like you.

Did you enjoy this book?
We would love to hear from you.

Please send your comments to:
Hallmark Book Feedback
P.O. Box 419034
Mail Drop 100
Kansas City, MO 64141

Or e-mail us at:
booknotes@hallmark.com